AF571943

A rhinoceros is a very large animal. This one weighs more than some automobiles. It is a peaceful animal, and usually rests during the day and eats at night.

Most rhinoceroses have two horns, but some have only one.

BIG & LITTLE ANIMALS

An Animal Information Book

by Elizabeth Elias Kaufman

THIRD PRINTING — JANUARY 1989

PRICE STERN SLOAN
Los Angeles

Prairie dogs are small animals. They have short legs and short tails. Their ears are very small and do not stick out very far from their heads.

When a prairie dog is in danger, it makes a lot of noise. This warns all the other prairie dogs.

Hamsters are such small animals that you could hold one in your hand. They are only five or six inches long, and weigh less than one half of a pound.

Camels have long legs and a long neck. Some camels, such as this dromedary, have one hump on their backs. Other types of camels have two humps.

Camels can go for several days without eating any food or drinking any water. When they need energy, camels use the fat that is stored in their hump (or humps).

An opossum is a little animal, about the same size as a house cat.

Opossums use their tails to hang from trees, and to carry things.

When it is frightened by another animal, the opossum falls down. The other animal thinks the opossum is dead and leaves it alone.

Polar bears are big animals. They can be up to eight or nine feet long. Even though they are big, these bears are excellent, graceful swimmers.

Polar bears have a heavy coat of white fur. They need a heavy coat because they live in very cold places like Canada and Alaska.

Koalas weigh only about thirty pounds. They are between two and two and a half feet long.

These animals live in trees, but only eat the leaves from eucalyptus trees.

Koalas live only in Australia.

A fully grown male lion, such as this one, weighs 400 or more pounds.

The long hair around a male lion's face is called a mane. Female lions do not have manes.

This little monkey weighs about five pounds. It is a Verved monkey. Verved monkeys eat many different kinds of fruits and vegetables.

This type of monkey lives on the ground and in trees.

A humpback whale, such as this one, is about fifty feet long. The flippers at the end of its body add another fifteen feet to the whale's length.

Although whales live in the water, they must come up to the surface to breathe.

This small animal is a ground squirrel. Its tail is not quite as bushy as a tree squirrel's.

Ground squirrels like to eat seeds and nuts.

Giraffes are very large animals. They are about nineteen feet tall.

Giraffes have two small horns on top of their heads.

A giraffe's tongue is very long and is used to pull leaves off of the tops of trees.

Raccoons are very good at climbing trees. They may spend the day sleeping and resting in a tree. At night, raccoons hunt for food.

Raccoons are small animals with long tails. Their tails have several rings of dark and light stripes.

Elephants are the largest animals that live on land.

There are two kinds of elephants, African elephants and Indian elephants. African elephants are larger than Indian elephants.

This is an African elephant. It is about eleven and a half feet tall.

There are many different types of rabbits. Most rabbits are very small. The largest type of rabbit weighs only about fifteen pounds.

Some rabbits live in woods and forests. Other rabbits, such as this French Lop, are pets.

Animal Information Books

Titles in this Series

Baby Animals
Baby Zoo Animals
Bears
Big & Little Animals
Birds
Bunnies & Rabbits
Butterflies
Farm Animals
Horses & Ponies
Kittens & Cats
Lions & Tigers
Monkeys & Apes
Penguins
Pets
Puppies & Dogs
Sea Animals
Wild Animals
Zoo Animals

Copyright © 1986 Ottenheimer Publishers, Inc.
Published by Price Stern Sloan, Inc.
360 North La Cienega Boulevard, Los Angeles, California 90048
All Rights Reserved.
ISBN: 0-8431-1522-X

Printed in Korea.